Shedagh Cummins

POPULAR
ANTIQUES
and their
VALUES

Compiled and Edited by
TONY CURTIS

1st	Edition	October 1971
2nd	Impression	November 1971
3rd	Impression	December 1971
4th	Impression	January 1972
5th	Impression	March 1972
6th	Impression	May 1972
7th	Impression	June 1972
8th	Impression	August 1972
2nd	Edition	August 1973 (Revised Prices)
2nd	Impression	December 1973
3rd	Impression	June 1974
4th	Impression	December 1974
3rd	Edition	June 1975 (Revised Prices)

LYLE PUBLICATIONS © 1971

GLENMAYNE   GALASHIELS   SELKIRKSHIRE   SCOTLAND

CONTENTS

Introduction	9
Monarchs	11
Periods	12
Registry of Designs	13
Bureaux	14
Bureau Bookcases	16
Barometers	18
Blackamoor figures and Torcheres	19
Beds and Cradles	20
Bookcases	22
Copper and Brass	24
Chairs	28
Couches	34
China	36
Chests and Tallboys	42
Commode Chests	44
Canterburys	46
Commodes	47
Clocks	48
Corner Cabinets	54
China cabinets and Vitrines	56
Chiffoniers and Credenzas	58
Dolls and Toys	60
Davenports	62
Dressers	64
Dressing tables	66
Escritoires	67
Glass	68
Lowboys	72
Military Chests	73
Musical Boxes and Automaton Figures	74
Models	75
Mirrors	76
Miscellanea	78
Pedestal & Kneehole Desks	82

Secretaires 84
Suites 86
Stools 87
Silver 88
Tables 94
Sideboards 102
Tea Caddies and Boxes 104
Trunks 106
Writing Tables 108
Work Boxes 110
Wine Coolers 112
Whatnots 113
Wardrobes and Cupboards 114
Chair Backs 116
Handles 118
Legs 120
Pediments 122
Index 123

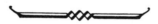

Printed in Great Britain by

APOLLO PRESS   DOMINION WAY   WORTHING   SUSSEX

INTRODUCTION

With the increase in popularity of Antiques and Antique Collecting a need has arisen for a comprehensive reference work of detailed illustrations and prices to be used as a guide to current market values.

The purpose of this publication is to make it easy for those either buying, selling, or merely interested in the value of the pieces in their own home, to identify and have a knowledge of the price an Antique Dealer is likely to pay for a piece in average condition.

The illustrations have been most carefully chosen to bring your attention to the significance of detail, which could appear to be an unimportant variation in style but may represent not only fifty years in age but fifty pounds in value. This being only one important factor to be taken into consideration when making an estimate of an average piece.

The condition of an Antique is of great importance. Most collectors and dealers will agree that it is the exception rather than the rule to find a piece of furniture that has not sustained damage or been altered in accordance with fashion at some time during its life. A tall piece may have had feet cut down, or a naturally light wood stained a darker shade and thereby spoiled. When a set of handles have been changed the original set are likely to be irreplaceable. A small piece of veneer missing may seem of little consequence but it will take the work of a craftsman to put it right which costs both time and money.

When making any calculations it is wise to remember that the dealer may have to spend as much having the piece put in a saleable condition as he has originally paid for that same item. One must also allow for his profit margin. At all times the cost of restoration must be taken into account, for even the most rare piece, if damaged is imperfect, and therefore of lesser value than the perfect example.

The current value of an Antique varies enormously in different areas. What is fashionable in one county may be totally disregarded in another which accounts for the amount of trading between dealers who come from different parts of the country. This will also happen when one dealer is more knowledgeable than another or a specialist in a particular field. One dealer may find it more profitable to turn his stock over frequently in order to keep his money 'working' for him and will therefore buy and sell while showing a very modest profit.

Another may treat his stock as an investment and can afford to wait for a higher price. Once a trend has been established in a particular period or style, the value will remain high for as long as that trend lasts. This can happen in a locality where overseas buyers make regular calls buying 'their' goods at 'their' price until they have completed a shipment, when the price will be revised in accordance with demand, and will probably return to normal.

With well over 1,300 illustrations we cover both the expensive collectors items and those, which although not in the true sense Antiques, are still much sought after in the Antique Trade, along with a price guide which having taken all relevant factors into account, is to the best of our knowledge a fair estimate of the price a dealer will pay for a piece in average condition. This will not be his selling price as has been explained.

We have had a great deal of help from private collectors and dealers during our research into this volume and wish to express our thanks to all concerned.

We wish you a smooth path in this exciting field.

TONY CURTIS

MONARCHS

HENRY 1V	1399 - 1413
HENRY V	1413 - 1422
HENRY V1	1422 - 1461
EDWARD 1V	1461 - 1483
EDWARD V	1483 - 1483
RICHARD 111	1483 - 1485
HENRY V11	1485 - 1509
HENRY V111	1509 - 1547
EDWARD V1	1547 - 1553
MARY	1553 - 1558
ELIZABETH	1558 - 1603
JAMES 1	1603 - 1625
CHARLES 1	1625 - 1649
COMMONWEALTH	1649 - 1660
CHARLES 11	1660 - 1685
JAMES 11	1685 - 1689
WILLIAM & MARY	1689 - 1695
WILLIAM 111	1695 - 1702
ANNE	1702 - 1714
GEORGE 1	1714 - 1727
GEORGE 11	1727 - 1760
GEORGE 111	1760 - 1820
GEORGE 1V	1820 - 1830
WILLIAM 1V	1830 - 1837
VICTORIA	1837 - 1901
EDWARD V11	1901 - 1910

PERIODS

TUDOR PERIOD	1485 - 1603
ELIZABETHAN PERIOD	1558 - 1603
INIGO JONES	1572 - 1652
JACOBEAN PERIOD	1603 - 1688
STUART PERIOD	1603 - 1714
A. C. BOULLE	1642 - 1732
LOUIS XIV PERIOD	1643 - 1715
GRINLING GIBBONS	1648 - 1726
CROMWELLIAN PERIOD	1649 - 1660
CAROLEAN PERIOD	1660 - 1685
WILLIAM KENT	1684 - 1748
WILLIAM & MARY PERIOD	1689 - 1702
QUEEN ANNE PERIOD	1702 - 1714
GEORGIAN PERIOD	1714 - 1820
T. CHIPPENDALE	1715 - 1762
LOUIS XV PERIOD	1723 - 1774
A. HEPPLEWHITE	1727 - 1788
ADAM PERIOD	1728 - 1792
ANGELICA KAUFMANN	1741 - 1807
T. SHERATON	1751 - 1806
LOUIS XVI	1774 - 1793
T. SHEARER	(circa) 1780
REGENCY PERIOD	1800 - 1830
EMPIRE PERIOD	1804 - 1815
VICTORIAN PERIOD	1830 - 1901
EDWARDIAN PERIOD	1901 - 1910

REGISTRY OF DESIGNS

USED 1842 to 1883

FOR EXAMPLE   12th Nov. 1852

1842 - 1867

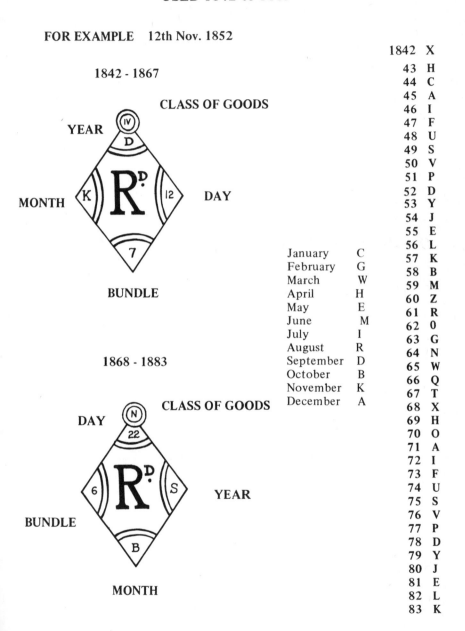

YEAR

CLASS OF GOODS

MONTH

DAY

BUNDLE

January	C
February	G
March	W
April	H
May	E
June	M
July	I
August	R
September	D
October	B
November	K
December	A

1868 - 1883

DAY

CLASS OF GOODS

YEAR

BUNDLE

MONTH

1842	X
43	H
44	C
45	A
46	I
47	F
48	U
49	S
50	V
51	P
52	D
53	Y
54	J
55	E
56	L
57	K
58	B
59	M
60	Z
61	R
62	O
63	G
64	N
65	W
66	Q
67	T
68	X
69	H
70	O
71	A
72	I
73	F
74	U
75	S
76	V
77	P
78	D
79	Y
80	J
81	E
82	L
83	K

FOR EXAMPLE 22nd Oct. 1875

18th century oak bureau with fluted pillars.   £190

Edwardian inlaid cylinder front bureau.   £160

Victorian carved oak bureau.   £100

Late 19th century lacquered bureau on bracket feet. £85

Sheraton style sandlewood bureau.   £275

Early 18th century oak bureau with stand.   £150

Edwardian mahogany bureau with shell inlay and bracket feet.   £75

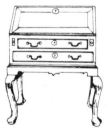

Early Georgian mahogany bureau on stand.   £400

Edwardian oak bureau on stretcher base.   £20

French mahogany bureau with inlaid flowers and ormolu mounts.   £400

Dutch marquetry bonheur-de-jour.   £575

Edwardian Sheraton style bureau with cylinder top and cupboard under. £120

Dutch mahogany bombe front, cylinder desk with shaped interior.   £600

French marquetry and rosewood bureau with brass gallery and cabriole legs. £255

Edwardian inlaid mahogany cylinder front bureau.   £140

Early 17th century oak bureau.   £450

William and Mary walnut veneered bureau. £2,300

Georgian mahogany bureau on splayed feet.   £245

Queen Anne bureau in walnut with herringbone banding.
£900

Queen Anne walnut bureau or stand.   £2,500

Edwardian inlaid mahogany bureau with cupboard under.   £75

Small George III mahogany bureau on ogee feet. £425

William and Mary walnut bureau on stand. £1,250

Small William and Mary oak bureau with shaped interior.
£350

George II style red
and gold lacquered
bureau bookcase.
£1,550

Georgian mahogany
bureau bookcase with
astragal glazed doors.
£600

Small 18th century
Dutch marquetry
bureau cabinet.
£2,300

Victorian mahogany
cylinder front bureau
bookcase.   £145

Edwardian oak bureau
bookcase with leaded
glazing.   £60

Edwardian inlaid mahog-
any bureau bookcase.
£220

Small Queen Anne
walnut bureau book-
case.   £4,750

Early 20th century
oak bureau bookcase.
£40

George II mahogany
bureau cabinet on
ogee feet.   £1,400

Hepplewhite period
bureau bookcase in
mahogany with latti-
ced glazed doors.
£2,750

17th century walnut
bureau bookcase with
Vauxhall mirror doors.
£3,000

Early 18th century
Flemish marquetry
bureau cabinet £2,400

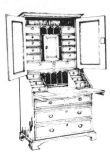

Queen Anne walnut bureau bookcase with a stepped interior £1,600

Mid 18th century bureau bookcase in mahogany. £900

Early 18th century walnut bureau bookcase with panelled doors. £2,250

Late 18th century mahogany bureau bookcase with glazed doors in the Gothic manner. £675

George II walnut bureau bookcase with double domed top. £1,750

Small Queen Anne bureau bookcase with the upper front having a moulded cornice and a bevelled mirror door. £6,000

Queen Anne walnut bureau bookcase with original mirrors and brasses. £2,350

Edwardian walnut bureau bookcase on cabriole leg supports. £95

Burr yew wood cylinder desk and bookcase with satinwood, kingwood and tulipwood enrichments. £7,000

Small George II red walnut bureau bookcase with original bevelled Vauxhall mirror door flanked by fluted pilasters. £2,750

George I yew wood bureau bookcase with broken arched pediment. £3,000

Edwardian Sheraton style cylinder front bureau bookcase with glazed doors. £325

17

BAROMETERS

Victorian oak framed
wall barometer. £8

Late Victorian baro-
meter in a carved oak
case. £18

Sheraton
period wheel
barometer.
£65

Victorian walnut
framed barometer with
moulded edge. £30

An early Victorian
rosewood cased banjo
barometer inlaid with
mother of pearl. £45

Victorian mahogany
tulip top barometer.
£35

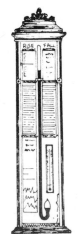

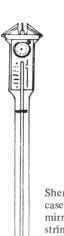

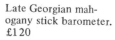

Sheraton mahogany
cased barometer with
mirror and boxwood
string inlay. £80

Georgian mahogany
cased barometer with
hygrometer, thermom-
eter and clock. £140

Georgian walnut cased
cistern pediment
barometer. £170

A Victorian Admiral
Fitzroy barometer in
an oak case. £35

Late Georgian mah-
ogany stick barometer.
£120

A small pair of early
19th century carved wood
blackamoor tables inlaid
with various woods, ivory
and pewter. 20 ins. high.
£350

A pair of early 19th
century Venetian black-
amoor figures in the form
of lamps 34 ins. high. £325

Early 19th century
blackamoor figure on stand.
6 ft. high.   £300

Fine pair of early 19th
century blackamoor figures
in attractive colours. 6ft.,
2ins. high.   £850

Regency period blackamoor
figure on stand. 5ft.8ins.high.
£375

French Empire black and
white marble column with
ormolu mounts.   £160

Regency period
rosewood torchere
with brass
mounts.   £120

Chippendale mah-
ogany torchere on
carved tripod
base.   £140

Georgian torchere with
rams head mounts and
hoof feet.   £95

19th century Dutch marquetry bed 3ft, wide. £210

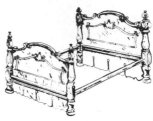

19th century red lacquer and gilt bed 4ft. wide, decorated with domestic scenes. £175

Late Victorian figured mahogany bed, 4ft. 6ins. wide. £25

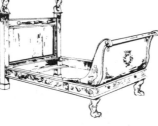

Regency mahogany bed with ormolu decoration and paw feet. £225

Italian carved walnut four poster bed. £310

Victorian brass bed 3ft wide. £50

A Victorian brass half tester bed 4ft. 6ins. wide. £100

17th century oak four poster bed. £360

Early Georgian mahogany tester with original drapes 4ft. 6ins. wide. £350

Early 19th century oak cot.   £45

Victorian wicker work cradle.   £12

Late Georgian suspended cot in canework on a mahogany stand. £70

Hepplewhite mahogany canework crib.   £100

Sheraton period crib with a mechanical rocker.   £150

17th century oak cradle   £75

19th century country made chair back crib in elm.   £60

A Victorian brass crib.   £65

Late 17th century oak hooded cradle.   £70

Victorian mahogany
standing bookcase.   £35

Edwardian mahogany
revolving bookcase inlaid
with bone and ivory. £65

Victorian mahogany hang-
ing shelves with small
drawer in the base. £35

Georgian mahogany book-
case with fluted columns.
£325

Victorian mahogany open
bookshelves.   £50

Regency brass inlaid rosewood bookcase. £340

Late Georgian mahogany
breakfront bookcase with
astragal glazed doors and
cupboards to base. £1,250

Chippendale mahogany
bookcase with carved cor-
nice and cluster column
pilasters.   £450

Victorian breakfront
bookcase in mahogany with
glazed doors enclosing adjustable shelves.   £500

Regency period open shelf brass inlaid bookcase in rosewood with marble top.   £220

Late Georgian satinwood bookcase having centre shelves flanked by cupboards.   £215

Small Regency mahogany bookcase on stand with a brass grille door.   £275

Georgian standing bookshelves in finely grained mahogany.   £275

Regency mahogany breakfront bookcase with brass grille to cupboard doors. £215

Regency period ebonised standing bookshelves having brass stringing and painted panels to cupboards and back.   £220

George III mahogany breakfront bookcase with satinwood stringing having adjustable shelves enclosed by astragal glazed doors. £6,500

Regency period Gothic style bookcase with glazed doors and cupboards enclosing drawers to base.   £225

Georgian mahogany breakfront bookcase with glazed doors to upper section and cupboards below. £1,300

Victorian copper kettle and stand. £20

A Bidri ware brass vase. £3

Late Victorian brass vase 10ins. high. £10

Victorian copper samovar. £30

A large Victorian two wheel coffee mill. £25

Victorian brass preserving pan, 15ins. diameter. £7

Victorian two gallon copper milk churn. £30

Victorian copper milk pail. £15

17th century bell metal skillet. £17.50

Victorian copper skillet with iron handle. £9

A 19th century copper log bin. £25

Victorian copper helmet coal scuttle. £25

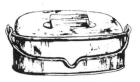

Victorian copper wash boiler. £18

19th century four gallon copper measure. £30

19th century small bronze howitzer. 12 ins. long. £110

An 18th century brass bucket. £100

A modern model of an early 19th century field cannon, 26ins. long. £65

Large Victorian bronze 'wooden wall' ships lantern, 45ins. high. £55

Georgian brass coal scuttle. £27

A Victorian brass trivet. £8

Victorian brass kettle. £8

An Art Nouveau copper jug 12 ins. high. £6

Victorian copper grape hod 35ins. high. £45

Large Georgian copper saucepan with lid. £18

Victorian brass milk can £7

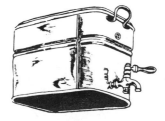

Victorian brass helmet coal scuttle. £12

Victorian copper urn with brass tap. £15

Victorian copper jardiniere. £15

Victorian brass carriage lamp. £20

Victorian ships mast lamp in brass. £25

Victorian brass oil lamp with white glass shade. £20

Victorian brass argand lamp. £40

Georgian brass trivet with turned wood handle. £7

Pair of Georgian brass candlesticks 8ins., high. £15

Edwardian brass cash till. £40

Victorian brass and iron fire dogs. £8

Victorian brass students lamp. £10

Victorian brass inkstand. £10

Victorian brass fire irons complete with stand. £22

Victorian brass magazine stand. £40

17th century brass, steel handled warming pan. £40

Victorian brass and copper standard lamp £65

Victorian ships lamp in copper. £18

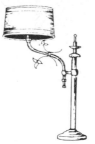

Victorian brass table lamp. £25

19th century brass table lamp. £28

Victorian brass hanging lamp with a green glass shade. £35

Victorian copper chafing dish. £12

Victorian brass Crystal Palace bird cage. £45

Large Georgian copper pan. £18

18th century copper urn with brass lid. £45

Georgian brass saucepan. £9

Georgian brass kettle. £12

Georgian copper warming pan. £30

Victorian brass cakestand. £16

Large pair of brass twist candlesticks. £15

Victorian brass candelabrum. £30

Late Victorian oak framed dining chair.
Set of 4 - £40
Set of 6 - £60

Early Victorian simulated rosewood bedroom chair with cane seat.
Set of 4 - £50
Set of 6 - £80

Late 19th century dining chair with brass ornamentation.
Set of 4 - £70
Set of 6 - £115

19th century elm kitchen chair.
Set of 4 - £20
Set of 6 - £30

19th century Windsor wheelback chair in beech.
Set of 4 - £30
Set of 6 - £55

Victorian cabriole leg dining chair in rosewood.
Set of 4 - £110
Set of 6 - £275

Early Victorian mahogany balloon back dining chair.
Set of 4 - £50
Set of 6 - £100

Victorian cabriole leg dining chair in walnut.
Set of 4 - £110
Set of 6 - £275

William IV mahogany frame dining chair upholstered in leather.
Set of 4 - £65
Set of 6 - £135

Hepplewhite period mahogany dining chair.
Set of 4 - £150
Set of 6 - £400

French rococo style dining chair in giltwood.
Set of 4 - £150
Set of 6 - £300

Hepplewhite period dining chair in mahogany.
Set of 4 - £150
Set of 6 - £400

Victorian mahogany
bar back chair on turned
legs.
Set of 4 - £70
Set of 6 - £125

Chippendale Gothic
style mahogany chair
on square legs with
stretchers.
Set of 4 - £300
Set of 6 - £750

Mid 18th century
mahogany servants
hall chair.
Single - £30
Pair - £75

Victorian splat back
kitchen chair in elm.
Set of 4 - £20
Set of 6 - £35

19th century Chippendale
style mahogany chair
with ball and claw feet.
Set of 4 - £150
Set of 6 - £300

Derbyshire oak dining
chair.
Single - £40
Pair - £90

Early 19th century
mahogany dining
chair on turned legs.
Set of 4 - £110
Set of 6 - £250

Regency mahogany
dining chair with 'X'
frame back.
Set of 4 - £150
Set of 6 - £325

Regency mahogany
dining chair with
cane seat and back
and sabre legs.
Set of 4 - £150
Set of 6 - £350

Charles II walnut
dining chair .
Single - £80
Pair -- £180

Regency period
mahogany dining
chair with scimi-
tar shaped legs.
Set of 4 - £125
Set of 6 - £285

Regency rope back
dining chair in rose-
wood with sabre legs.
Set of 4 - £200
Set of 6 - £500

Regency mahogany childs chair and stand.   £60

Ebonised wood, rush seated Shetland chair. £25

Late Georgian Windsor wheel back armchair in yew wood.   £70

Windsor wheelback childs high chair in elm.   £25

Hepplewhite period mahogany elbow chair on fine tapered legs.   £75

Hepplewhite shield and feathers back elbow chair in mahogany.   £80

Regency X back mahogany elbow chair on sabre legs.   £65

Edwardian inlaid mahogany elbow chair on square tapering legs with spade feet.   £20

Fine Hepplewhite period armchair on tapering legs with stretchers.   £110

William IV dining chair upholstered in brown hide.   £35

William IV mahogany elbow chair on turned legs.   £35

Regency period ebonised elbow chair with splayed legs.   £70

Charles II walnut
high chair. £350

Victorian smokers
chair in elm. £12

Yorkshire ladder
back armchair in
elm and oak. £25

Jacobean oak hall
chair carved with
scrolls and con-
ventional floral
ornament. £120

Hepplewhite style
mahogany wheel
back elbow chair.
£45

Edwardian inlaid
mahogany corner
chair. £25

Hepplewhite mahogany
spindle back elbow
chair. £75

Sheraton period
painted armchair.
£125

Victorian papier mache
salon chair. £85

18th century padouk
wood armchair. £130

George I walnut
veneered armchair.
on carved cabriole
legs with ball and
claw feet. £425

Queen Anne black
japanned chair with
caned seat and back.
£575

Edwardian ebonised horseshoe back chair. £16

Victorian nursing chair upholstered in original bead and needlework cover. £65

Victorian walnut Preiu Dieu chair on cabriole leg supports. £35

Edwardian inlaid walnut nursing chair. £40

Victorian Preiu Dieu chair supported on turned legs. £25

Victorian walnut ladies chair with original tapestry cover. £85

Victorian balloon back ladies chair on cabriole leg supports. £90

Victorian walnut frame horseshoe back smokers chair. £25

Victorian iron frame chair on turned legs. £35

Hepplewhite period Gainsborough chair upholstered in green hide. £450

French Empire giltwood elbow chair. £125

Georgian Bergere chair in satinwood. £130

Victorian Abbotsford chair in walnut.   £35

Small Victorian buttoned sewing chair.   £35

Late Victorian arm-chair.   £16

Victorian mahogany cabriole leg grand-father chair.   £100

Regency library chair with original leather cover.   £140

Victorian rosewood gents chair.   £75

French fauteuil in carved giltwood with original tap-estry cover.   £125

Georgian manogany library chair with sliding writing com-partment.   £235

Victorian mahogany block arm grandfather chair on turned legs.   £60

George II mahogany armchair on cluster column legs. £425

Queen Anne winged easy chair.   £350

Chippendale period mahogany arm-chair on carved cabriole legs. £425

Edwardian inlaid mahogany
settee on square tapering
legs.   £45

Victorian ottoman on
turned leg supports.
£200

Victorian scroll end
mahogany sofa on
turned legs.   £70

Late Victorian mahogany
framed love seat on turned
leg supports.   £95

Victorian couch with
carved mahogany frame
on turned legs.   £85

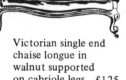

Victorian single end
chaise longue in
walnut supported
on cabriole legs. £125

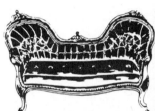

Victorian sofa in
walnut on cabriole
legs.   £250

Georgian mahogany
settee on cabriole
legs.   £270

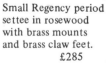

Small Regency period
settee in rosewood
with brass mounts
and brass claw feet.
£285

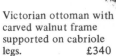

Hepplewhite period
mahogany settee.   £330

Victorian ottoman with
carved walnut frame
supported on cabriole
legs.   £340

Edwardian ebonised
settee on tapered
legs.   £25

Victorian mahogany
framed sofa.   £160

Early Victorian walnut
framed buttoned couch
on cabriole legs. £140

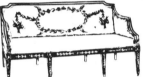

Hepplewhite period
settee on tapered legs.
£365

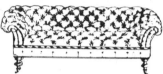

Victorian two seater
chesterfield.   £50

Regency period mahogany
framed settee with sabre
legs.   £230

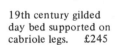

19th century gilded
day bed supported on
cabriole legs.   £245

William IV mahogany
salon sofa.   £140

17th century oak
settee.   £225

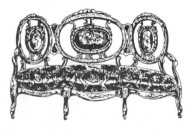

Victorian papier mache
sofa inlaid with mother
of pearl.   £325

Early carved oak hall
seat in elm.   £160

Staffordshire figure of
Lieutenant Hector
Munro being carried
off by a tiger.   £360

Royal Dux figure of
a child with dog.
7½ins.high.   £45

Victorian parian
figure.   £22

Staffordshire figure of
the young Queen
Victoria.   £75

Staffordshire figure of
Shakespeare, 18ins. high.
£40

Leeds creamware
seated Sphinx.
c.1770.   £140

Victorian parian figure
14ins.,high.   £22

A 6th century B.C. green
glaze ushabji.   £40

Capo di Monte group
'The Declaration' by
Guiseppe Gricci. £12,000

Victorian Staffordshire
flat back.   £17

Victorian monkey band
figure.   £22

19th century Staffordshire
castle.   £24

Victorian fairing 'The last in
bed to put out the light'. £22

Staffordshire group showing a man being trampled by a horse. £550

A T'ang Dynasty horse. £17,000

Bow porcelain figure of the infant Bachus and a leopard. 1750.   £255

Doulton brown salt glaze figure of Lord Nelson. £85

18th century bust of Minerva by Ralph Wood. £105

An early Victorian nodding figure. £25

A MennecyMagot figure.   £840

19th century Derby figure.   £80

Staffordshire flat back figure.   £18

Late 18th century Staffordshire pottery figure of birds.   £230

Staffordshire cottage figure.   £140

18th century Staffordshire figure of a duck.   £250

19th century Staffordshire cottage.   £25

37

19th century
Prattware vase.
£30

Wedgwood three
colour vase. £200

Victorian Goss
china vase. £1.50

Small Victorian
yellow ground vase.
£3

Victorian vase 15ins.
high.   £6

A T'ang Dynasty jar
with a finely cracked
pale greyish glaze.
£1,000

Wedgwood and Bentley
vase and cover. £950

Small Victorian
Wedgwood vase.
£8

A Doulton Queen
Victoria commemor-
ative jug.   £18

Victorian shaving mug.
£4

A blue and white Caughley
jug.   £27

A Dr. Wall Worcester
hot water jug and cover
probably painted in
the atelier of James
Giles.   £850

A blue and brown
Derby plate. £22

Sevres porcelain plaque
'La Recreation des
Moissonneurs' forming
the top of a Louis XV
table.   £10,000

A creamware black
transfer octagonal
plate.   £16

Early 19th century
Worcester teapoy. £35

19th century Belleek
jardinier.   £45

A Cologne ovoid
vase. £45

A Victorian vase with
bird decoration 10 ins
high.   £7

A 16th century Chinese
Kinrande double gourd
vase.   £28,000

A Benjamin Lunds vase
7½ ins. high.   £875

Doulton vase
12ins high. £15

Minton vase draped with
swans.   £22

Large Victorian jug. £10

Victorian lustre
jug.   £15

A Ming period white
porcelain ewer
            £14,000

Copeland and Garret
jug 1845.   £14

A Hans Sloane pattern
red anchor Chelsea
plate.   £1,500

Victorian Staffordshire
plaque.   £15

19th century green
Wedgwood plate. £3

A Victorian chamber pot. £3

Victorian jug and basin set. £7

An 18th century Chinese porcelain punch bowl. £1,350

19th century Imari bowl. 9ins. diameter. £12

A 19th century blue and white foot bath. £18

A Sunderland lustre punch bowl. 12ins., diameter. £35

Victorian feeding cup. £3

Leeds creamware mug. 8ins.high., 1770. £300

Victorian Goss china mug. £3

Whieldon tortoiseshell teapot. £625

A Victorian Cadogan teapot. £25

Wedgwood octagonal teapot. £150

A Ch'ien Lung ground Canton fish tank. 18 ins. diameter. £140

Victorian china slop pail. £5

Minton majolica pot. £6

A Marseilles faience tureen and cover from the Veuve Perrin factory £500

A Cheng Te period Ming Imperial yellow bowl. £3,000

A 19th century Wedgwood biscuit barrel with silver lid. £30

1937 Coronation Mug. £4

Wedgwood blue and white jasper tulip pot. £300

A Liverpool mug painted in famille rose colours. £100

A Newhall teapot. £35

Staffordshire salt glaze 'King of Prussia' teapot. £180

Wedgwood three colour dice-pattern teapot. £235

Victorian Wellington chest veneered in rosewood.   £110

Victorian stripped pine chest of drawers on turned feet.   £25

Dutch oak bombe chest 3ft. wide.   £280

William and Mary walnut chest 3ft. 2ins. wide. £400

William and Mary cabinet with walnut oyster veneer and barley twist legs with cross stretchers.   £800

Period oak chest of drawers on bun feet.   £190

Dutch marquetry tallboy with frieze drawer. £375

18th century mahogany tallboy with brass capitals and carved cornice. £250

Georgian mahogany tallboy with Chinese lattice work frieze.   £375

Small Georgian bow front chest of drawers in well figured mahogany with a flush caddy top and splayed feet, 2ft. 9ins. wide. £220

Victorian mahogany chest of drawers with barley twist columns to the front edge. £15

Queen Anne bachelors chest in walnut 2ft. 7ins. wide. £1,500

George I walnut chest of four long drawers, with brushing slide and wide crossbanding. £500

Queen Anne walnut chest on stand with oak lined drawers. £540

Sheraton satinwood bow fronted chest, crossbanded in tulipwood with ebony and boxwood stringing, with a brushing slide. £1,100

Victorian mahogany tallboy on splay feet, with boxwood stringing. £130

George I crossbanded walnut tallboy having a Norwich Sunburst decoration 3ft. 7ins. wide. £850

18th century walnut tallboy with fluted pilasters to the top section. £800

Inlaid bombe shape commode with grey marble top. 3ft 5ins. wide. £425

19th century French commode inlaid with floral marquetry. £475

Georgian shaped front inlaid satinwood commode. £2,000

Hepplewhite shaped front commode in satinwood with doors inlaid with panels of bamboo plant designs. £6,500

Small French marquetry commode. £300

Small Italian walnut commode inlaid with satinwood. £410

Georgian serpentine front commode in mellow mahogany. £600

Louis XV petite commode in kingwood and rosewood with ormolu mounts. £1,000

18th century French Provencal double serpentine front commode in walnut. £310

17th century commode
in walnut and holly. £900

Late Georgian semi
circular commode in
satinwood inlaid with
bows and ribbons. £575

18th century Dutch mar-
quetry commode in yew
wood.   £700

Dutch marquetry walnut
commode with bombe
front and sides.   £650

Small Louis XV style
marquetry commode
on cabriole shaped
supports.   £425

19th century kingwood
marquetry and parquetry
commode.   £560

French commode in
kingwood and tulip-
wood with rose marble
top and ormolu decor-
ation.   £1,000

18th century serpentine
shaped commode of
three long drawers inlaid
with various woods and
rouge marble top.   £900

Georgian serpentine front
commode in satinwood
decorated with musical
instruments and ribbons.
£1,250

Small Victorian burr
walnut canterbury.   £80

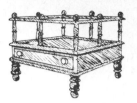

Late Victorian ebonised
canterbury with gilt
decoration.   £40

Regency mahogany
canterbury on fine
turned legs.   £110

Regency mahogany
canterbury with
drawer.   £110

Regency mahogany
canterbury on short
turned legs with brass
castors.   £130

Victorian rosewood
canterbury with drawer
to base.   £80

Georgian mahogany
canterbury on fine
turned feet terminating
in brass castors.   £120

Victorian burr walnut
music canterbury with
fretted supports and
drawer to base.   £110

Unusual Georgian mahogany
canterbury with drawer to
base.   £145

Small Victorian mahogany
one step commode.   £6

Victorian commode in
walnut with a pull out
step.   £12

Late Georgian mahogany
commode with lift up top
and dummy drawers.
                     £35

Georgian mahogany
commode on short
square legs.   £40

Regency night commode
in figured mahogany on
fine turned legs.   £85

Victorian three step
commode in mahogany.
                     £60

Regency bedroom cupboard
in mahogany inlaid with
satinwood.   £55

Georgian tray top night
table in satinwood inlaid
with kingwood.   £155

Georgian mahogany tray
top commode.   £75

CLOCKS

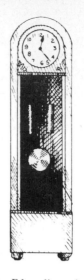

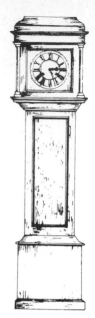

A late Georgian painted face oak case eight day grandfather clock. £100

An Edwardian oak case grandfather clock with glass panelled door. £60

19th century Continental grandfather clock. £200

A George III oak cased grandfather clock with square brass face. £170

An early 18th century longcase clock in a fine burr walnut case. 7ft., high. £725

An 18th century longcase clock in mahogany with a fretted door. £375

An early German grandfather clock. £175

A late 18th century mahogany longcase clock with a brass silvered dial. £275

Charles II longcase clock in figured walnut case.   £850

Late 17th century Dutch marquetry longcase clock.   £1,350

Late Georgian figured mahogany longcase clock.   £300

17th century marquetry cased clock by Marwick. £1100

Chippendale figured mahogany longcase clock with a brass face.   £675

Sheraton period mahogany cased grandfather clock inlaid with satinwood.   £450

William and Mary period walnut and marquetry longcase clock by Joseph Buckingham.   £1,400

19th century French boulle clock and pedestal 7ft. 9ins. tall.   £1,600

Late 19th century black marble mantel clock. £8

Victorian mahogany cased wall clock. £40

Late Victorian inlaid mahogany mantel clock. £12

A Victorian 'Big Ben' picture clock. £40

A 19th century American clock in a rosewood case. £22

A late 17th century bracket clock with a verge movement and engraved backplate. £450

Regency period bracket clock in an ebonised case inlaid with brass. £90

A late 18th century bracket clock in an ebonised pearwood case. £150

A Victorian chiming bracket clock. £75

A fine ebony veneered bracket clock by Joseph Knibb. £7,000

An Edwardian mahogany cased bracket clock with an enamel dial. £40

19th century cuckoo
clock in a mahogany
case.   £40

Regency period mantel
clock in brass inlaid mahogany case.   £50

An early 18th century
three train quarter chime
bracket clock.   £475

An ebonised bracket
clock by James Cowan
of Edinburgh.   £550

An early 18th century
brass lantern clock. £275

A George III bracket
clock 20ins.high, by
Stephen Rimbault of
London.   £1,250

Early 19th century bracket
clock with brass face and
engraved backplate.£200

A Victorian lancet
case clock.   £70

An early Victorian mantel
clock in a carved mahogany
case.   £40

A mid 19th century
ebonised bracket clock.
                            £200

A fine bracket clock by Edward
East 1602-1697.   £8,000

Late 18th century Continental brass mantel clock. £100

Louis XV Cartel clock in ormolu and tortoiseshell by Perache of Paris. £500

Victorian brass mantel clock surmounted with a cherub. £40

A French brass carriage clock in serpentine shaped case. £110

19th century brass mantel clock. £75

A 19th century French mantel clock by Leroy et Cie of Paris. 2ft. 2ins. High. £550

19th century French ormolu and tortoiseshell mantel clock. £150

A Regency period 'Father Time' clock in bronze and ormolu. £175

A French Empire style white marble and ormolu clock. £90

Louis XVI style ormolu clock with sevres plaques. £160

19th century alabaster mantel clock. £50

A Victorian brass cased clock and barometer. £60

19th century French mantel clock in a green lacquered case. £125

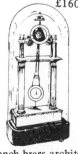

French brass architectural clock, 1810. £110

A Louis Phillipe ormolu clock with sevres panels. £185

A late Georgian wall clock in a mahogany case. £35

Early 19th century fusee movement wall clock with a quarter strike by Hampson of London. £100

A Victorian steeple clock in a mahogany case. £16

A fine Viennese enamel table clock 11ins. high. £525

Small 19th century brass carriage clock with an alarm. £75

19th century skeleton clock under a glass dome. £105

A French maritime clock in ormolu on a rouge marble base. £155

19th century gilded spelter mantel clock £20

A Louis XVI marble and ormolu clock by Piolane of Paris 22ins., high. £320

A 19th century brass lantern clock. £45

A French singing bird carriage clock 10ins. high. £1,100

An early 19th century French striking mantel clock. £75

Fine French carriage clock with alarm and repeater. £350

53

CORNER CABINETS

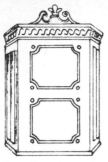

Late Georgian mahogany corner cupboard.   £80

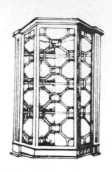

Early 18th century hanging display cabinet with astragal glazed doors and fluted pilasters.
£125

Late Georgian walnut veneered corner cupboard.   £140

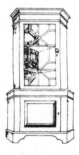

Edwardian mahogany corner cupboard. £100

Sheraton period mahogany corner cupboard with satinwood inlay.
£400

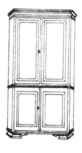

Late Georgian mahogany corner cupboard on ogee feet.   £145

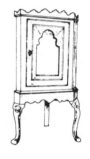

18th century walnut corner cupboard supported on carved cabriole legs.   £175

Chippendale mahogany corner cupboard with astragal glazed doors enclosing adjustable shelves.   £375

Georgian mahogany corner cupboard with centre drawer and astragal glazed doors.
£325

18th century oak dole cupboard with centre drawer and four shelves.   £125

Georgian mahogany corner cupboard with astragal glazed doors.   £250

Early 18th century black japanned corner cupboard decorated with domestic scenes. £100

George I walnut veneered corner cupboard with mirrored doors. £150

Georgian bow front mahogany corner cupboard with pear drop moulding. £140

Late Georgian standing corner cupboard in oak. £95

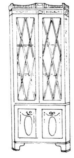

Late Georgian mahogany diamond glazed corner cupboard with satinwood inlay. £325

Early Georgian walnut corner cupboard on stand with centre drawer. £350

Queen Anne walnut standing corner cupboard. £400

Edwardian inlaid mahogany corner cupboard with inlaid conche shell to the lower section. £150

Georgian stripped pine corner cupboard. £125

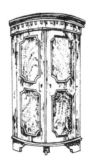

Late Georgian finely grained mahogany bow fronted corner cupboard. £150

George II bow fronted corner cupboard in mahogany. £375

Edwardian inlaid mahogany china cabinet with glazed doors. £75

Edwardian mahogany display cabinet. £55

19th century Venetian walnut display cabinet with carved decoration. £400

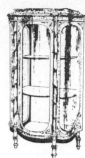

19th century gilt display cabinet with glass shelves. £300

19th century black and red boulle , ormolu mounted display cabinet. £180

Edwardian inlaid mahogany specimen table on tapered legs. £75

Victorian walnut music cabinet with brass gallery. £35

19th century boulle credenza with ormolu mounts. £550

Sheraton period inlaid satinwood hanging display cabinet. £215

Victorian walnut display cabinet inlaid with flowers. £150

19th century Dutch marquetry bombe shaped display cabinet. £2,000

Hepplewhite period display cabinet in satinwood. £2,250

Edwardian inlaid mahogany display cabinet on tapered legs. £205

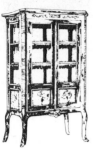

19th century French mahogany and tulipwood display cabinet inlaid with flowers. £350

19th century French display cabinet veneered in Kingwood with ormolu decoration. £340

Victorian display cabinet in Kingwood with Vernis Martin panels. £425

French walnut display cabinet inlaid with ebony. £165

Regency period ebonised display cabinet with figured marble top. £140

19th century marquetry display cabinet. £160

Georgian ebonised display cabinet with ormolu decoration. £175

Victorian burr walnut breakfront credenza. £450

Small Edwardian inlaid mahogany specimen display cabinet. £70

Victorian inlaid burr walnut credenza. £410

Chinese style Georgian mahogany display cabinet. £470

19th century display cabinet veneered in Kingwood with ormolu decoration. £450

Louis Philippe cabinet with Vernis Martin panels. £1,750

Victorian mahogany chiffonier with rococo carving. £65

Fine Regency chiffonier in rosewood. £320

Victorian mahogany chiffonier with panelled cupboard doors. £50

Late Victorian mahogany chiffonier with single drawer and cupboard below. £20

Regency cabinet in rosewood with brass inlaid frieze drawer and brass grille to the doors. £310

Regency chiffonier in rosewood with paw feet. £300

Regency rosewood chiffonier with brass grille to the doors and reeded columns. £240

Small Regency brass inlaid chiffonier with brass grille to the door. 2ft.wide. £275

Regency mahogany chiffonier with brass grille doors and gallery. £275

Regency mahogany buffet with brass string inlay and cupboard doors lined with green silk. £180

Victorian mahogany chiffonier with carved mouldings and white marble top. £65

Georgian concave side cupboard of finely figured mahogany. £300

Regency brass inlaid rosewood chiffonier with panelled doors. £210

Early Victorian rosewood chiffonier with panelled cupboard doors. £70

Regency mahogany cabinet with mirror panels to cupboard doors. £200

Regency brass inlaid chiffonier in rosewood. £325

Late Victorian walnut dressing table on cabriole leg front supports. £30

Regency chiffonier in figured mahogany £160

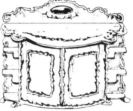

Regency bookshelves with brass grilles to the doors. £240

Victorian burr walnut credenza with centre cupboards flanked by open shelves. £150

Regency mahogany chiffonier with a figured marble top. £220

Georgian chiffonier in satinwood. £350

Regency mahogany bookcase crossbanded in satinwood. £275

Victorian figured mahogany chiffonier £70

59

DOLLS & TOYS

An early doll with muslin frock, and wool wig. £65

Victorian dolls house 31 x 14 x 45 ins. £65

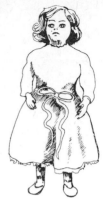

Simon and Halbig doll 28ins. high. £35

19th century doll with original clothing. £30

Dignified doll of the late Napolean III period. £200

Fine 19th century model of a horse drawn fire engine 15ins. long £50

Victorian wooden horse drawn caravan 28ins. long. £35

A Victorian rocking horse. £75

Victorian china doll. £25

60

Late 19th century
doll.   £20

A rare French doll
stamped Mme Roh-
mer.   £410

Doll made by Armand
Marseille in 1891.
                    £20

A Jumeau doll with
original clothes. £45

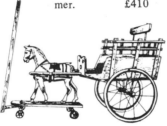

An early Victorian
wooden pony and
trap.   £55

Victorian doll with
original clothes. £30

Fine Victorian doll
with original clothes.
          £75

An early oak cat
kennel.   £45

Late 17th century
carved and painted
wooden rocking
horse.   £610

19th century model
of a railway signal
box.   £40

Edwardian inlaid
mahogany davenport
with cupboard under.
£80

William IV mahogany
davenport.   £130

Victorian inlaid wal-
nut davenport on
twist supports with
two shelves under. £55

Victorian davenport
veneered in burr walnut.
£160

William IV mahogany
davenport.   £150

Victorian burr walnut davenport
with cabriole leg front supports.
£175

Victorian cylindrical
davenport in burr
walnut.   £300

Victorian burr walnut
piano top davenport
with cupboard enc-
losing four drawers. £300

Chinese Chippendale style
mahogany davenport. £100

Victorian burr walnut serpentine
fronted davenport.   £200

Regency period rosewood
davenport on fluted legs.
£285

Oriental hardwood davenport
ornately carved with figures
and animals.   £130

Edwardian red mahogany davenport with cupboard enclosing four drawers. £85

Edwardian inlaid mahogany davenport on tapered legs with cross stretchers. £65

Victorian walnut davenport. £110

George III mahogany sliding top davenport on bracket feet. £300

William IV mahogany davenport with pillar supports. £130

Regency davenport veneered in satinwood with sliding top and pierced brass gallery. £300

Small Regency period davenport with oak lined drawers. £300

Regency mahogany sliding top davenport with four drawers. £300

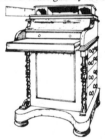

Victorian burr walnut piano top davenport with rising top. £285

19th century teak military desk and stand. £125

Regency period writing desk and bookshelves in rosewood. £190

Regency rosewood davenport with sliding top and scroll feet. £260

17th century Welsh
dresser in oak 8ft,
long.   £450

Small Georgian oak
Welsh dresser with
original plate racks
4ft. 7ins. wide. £300

Unusually small
Georgian oak dresser
with pot board. 35
ins. wide.   £325

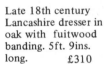

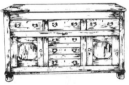

Late 18th century
Lancashire dresser in
oak with fuitwood
banding. 5ft. 9ins.
long.   £310

Early 18th century
oak dresser with cen-
tral cupboard.   £220

Late Georgian oak
dresser 5ft. 7ins.
wide.   £200

Early Georgian oak dresser
with pot board.   £350

Late 17th century oak
dresser 5ft. 11ins. wide.
£320

Late 18th century oak
dresser with pot board. £275

Georgian oak dresser only
4ft.5ins. long.   £340

Early Georgian oak
dresser.   £310

James II oak dresser on
baluster turned legs with
stretchers.   £500

Early 18th century polished
oak dresser on ogee
feet.   £310

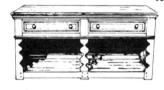

17th century oak dresser
with pot board.   £260

18th century oak dresser with
spice drawers. 6ft.long.   £285

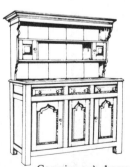

Georgian oak dresser with
fielded panels to cupboard
doors.   £340

Late 18th century oak
dresser with drawers and
cupboards to base. 5ft.,
long.   £340

George II Lancashire oak
dresser.   £425

Sheraton mahogany
corner washstand
with a centre cup-
board. £85

Georgian mahogany
dressing table with
an adjustable mirror.
£300

Late Georgian mah-
ogany washstand with
a centre drawer. £40

Edwardian inlaid
mahogany washstand
on square tapered legs.
£15

Victorian pine wash-
stand with a marble
top and tiled splash-
back.   £15

Victorian mahogany
washstand on a stret-
cher base.   £25

Sheraton washstand
with cistern, in
mahogany with box-
wood stringing. £110

Sheraton period
folding top dres-
sing table in satin-
wood. £225

Georgian mahogany
toilet cabinet.   £90

Victorian mahogany
escritoire on bun
feet. £130

William and Mary
secretaire cabinet
with floral marq-
uetry in stained
and natural woods.
£1,100

Dutch marquetry escri-
toire with fall front
enclosing drawers and
pigeon holes. £400

William and Mary
period walnut
escritoire. £900

18th century laburnum
wood chest on chest.
£1,000

French Empire
ladies escritoire
in mahogany. £325

Inlaid secretaire a
abattant with fall
front concealing
small drawers. £550

Small amboyna wood
escritoire on stand with
a writing slide. £275

Reproduction French
style escritoire with
Sevres plaques and
ormolu mounts
£350

GLASS

Victorian opal glass vase 10ins. high. £12

Late Georgian cut glass decanter. £14

Georgian cut glass decanter. £24

Georgian decanter. £10

A Cranberry glass water jug. £16

An Edwardian silver mounted claret jug. £55

A Georgian cut glass water jug. £24

A Mary Gregory glass pitcher 8ins. high. £20

A Burmese glass jug 4ins.high. £40

19th century green glass wine bottle. £10

A Victorian glass pickle jar. £2

A Mildner tumbler. £650

Victorian red glass lustre. £20

19th century glass biscuit barrel. £7

A Mamluk enamelled glass Mosque lamp in the name of Sultan Malik Zahir Barkuk AD1382-1399. £5,500

An 18th century Bristol five bottle cruet. £1,650

A Mary Gregory glass decanter. **£22**

A Lutz glass jug. **£38**

A Tiffany Favrille vase in iridescent golden glass. **£210**

Victorian satin glass vase 7ins. high. **£15**

19th century opal glass vase **£5**

Victorian Bohemian glass flask. **£30**

A Victorian claret jug with plated mounts. **£25**

A decorative Victorian glass vase 6ins. high. **£6**

19th century Cranberry glass jug. **£15**

An orange Carnival glass vase. **£3**

A Victorian red glass spill vase. **£5**

An early Georgian wine bottle 10ins. high. **£15**

Silver plated decanter stand, holding three cut glass bottles. **£60**

A Victorian cut glass centrepiece. **£35**

Victorian rosewood tantalus with brass mounts containing three cut glass decanters. **£55**

A Victorian Cranberry glass fruit and flower epergne. **£35**

GLASS

Vaseline glass scent
bottle.   £15

18th century wine
glass with an en-
graved bowl. £450

A Victorian glass
spill vase.   £5

A superb baluster
wine glass. £450

A glass bowl by
Gabriel Argy-
Rousseau   £135

Small Victorian
coloured glass bowl.
£6

A milk glass crim-
ped bowl.   £8

18th Century engraved
wine glass.   £110

Double ended
blue overlay scent
bottle with silver
tops.   £20

18th century wine
glass.   £100

Victorian red glass
scent bottle with
a silver top.   £18

A mother of pearl
snuff bottle. £65

A St. Louis green
carpet ground
paperweight. £1,250

Chinese snuff
bottle. £60

18th century baluster
wine glass. £125

Victorian opal glass
vase 4ins. high. £5

Victorian wine glass
red.   £ 3.50
blue.   £2.50
green. £ 2.00

A Tiffany scent
bottle.   £400

A rare Art Nouveau
glass inkwell
        £275

A Victorian water-
ing glass.   £5

Small Victorian col-
oured glass bowl.
        £4

Victorian satin glass
fruit and flower
epergne.   £25

18th century funnel
bowl wine glass. £135

A blue,gilt and enamel
scent bottle with a
gilt top.   £30

A baluster wine glass
with a trumpet bowl.
        £110

Chinese overlay glass
snuff bottle. £175

A St. Louis fuchsia
paperweight. £850

A Peking glass snuff
bottle with red over-
lay in the form of
flowers. £65

William and Mary
oak dressing table.
£190

Early 18th century mah-
ogany dressing table on
squared cabriole legs.
£165

George I walnut dres-
sing table on cabriole
legs.   £310

Georgian country made
lowboy in oak.
£115

Georgian country made
dressing table in fruit-
wood.   £105

George I lowboy in
figured walnut.
£365

Queen Anne lowboy
in fruitwood sup-
ported on cabriole
legs.   £450

William and Mary
dressing table in
walnut with arched
frieze and turned
legs with cross
stretchers.
£260

George II oak dres-
sing table on squar-
ed cabriole legs.
£155

Early 19th century mahogany military chest with a secretaire drawer.　£195

Victorian mahogany seamans chest with sunken wooden handles.　£80

19th century military chest with brass straps and corners and iron carrying handles.　£155

Camphor wood military chest with a secretaire drawer.　£235

Mahogany military chest with brass straps and corners and sunken wooden knobs.　£130

19th century mahogany military chest with a secretaire drawer.　£190

Early 19th century teak military chest with brass straps and sunken handles.　£180

Campaign chest in camphor wood with a helmet drawer and paw feet.　£240

19th century camphor wood secretaire military chest with an adjustable writing slope.　£285

19th century poly-
phone in a walnut case.
£200

A Victorian penny in
the slot polyphone.
£850

A Victorian Swiss
musical box in a
rosewood case. £170

An Edison Standard
phonograph. £70

A late 19th century
gramophone with a
fine brass horn. £55

A Victorian musical
box by Robert
F. Knoeloch play-
ing ten airs. £285

A 19th century French automaton group depicting a
barbers shop. £725

A 19th century sing-
ing bird in a cage
£250

An animated snake
dancer with a
musical movement by
Decamps of Paris.
£1,100

A 19th century automated
Spanish dancer. £425

A Victorian anim-
ated bisque
headed doll. £300

Prisoner of War bone
model of H.M.S.Mars
£1,400

A working model of
a piston with flywheel.
£25

French Prisoner of War
model of the frigate
Venus circa 1815.
£660

19th century scale model of
a steam tug.   £180

A model of the North
Eastern 1849 type Kitson
Thompson and Hewitson
Leeds 2.4.0. Locomotive.
£410

A coal fired working model
of the old LMS locomotive
Highland Chief.   £250

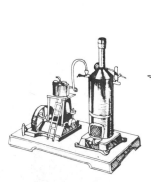

Model of a vertical
stationary steam engine
13ins. high.   £45

A Victorian model of a galleon.

£20

A 19th century coal fired
model steam engine 13½ins.
high.   £70

Victorian carved mahogany swing mirror. £15

Georgian mahogany wall mirror £75

Regency giltwood mirror surmounted by a carved eagle £95

Late Georgian gilded, Adam style wall mirror. £80

19th century Spanish gilded mirror. £85

Louis XVI carved giltwood mirror. £115

A Hepplewhite style mahogany toilet mirror. £45

Late Victorian walnut dressing table mirror. £8

Late Victorian mahogany swing mirror. £7

Late Georgian mahogany swing mirror. £35

Late Georgian vase shaped mahogany swing mirror. £50

Late Georgian cheval mirror. £60

Victorian gilded mantel mirror. £25

Large 19th century gilt mirror 15ft. x 4ft. £175

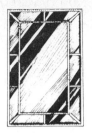

Chippendale period wall mirror with bird decoration. £180

18th century carved giltwood mirror. £90

Adam style gilt girandole. £60

Georgian carved and gilded mirror. £140

Georgian giltwood mirror with gesso ornamentation. £60

Early 19th century Spanish gilded mirror. £75

19th century white and gilded pine mirror. £70

Queen Anne lacquered toilet mirror on a bureau box base. £250

Victorian mahogany dressing table mirror. £14

Early Georgian mahogany swing mirror. £65

Late Georgian serpentine front mahogany swing mirror. £70

Early Victorian gilt wall mirror with gesso decoration. £40

Regency period gilded Pier glass and table. £225

Late Victorian mahogany cheval mirror. £40

Victorian metronome in an oak case.   £6

26th Dynasty bronze statue of a cat. £1,750

Victorian brass microscope in an oak case.   £45

A small 19th century German carved wood tankard. £15

A four case inro. £130

A bronze mare and foal by Isadore Bonheur. £750

Victorian chromatic stereoscope. £9

A 19th century oak Peg tankard. £40

Small pair of 18th century bellows. £10

Victorian turned wood tabacco jar. £6

Louis XV1 ormolu mounted ivory vase by Pierre Gouthlore.   £2,250

An ivory figure of a rat.   £135

An Infernal Harp shell from the Fringing Reef, Mauritius. £45

A five case inro. £260

Carved wood and ivory figure signed Yoshiaki, 9ins high.   £135

Late 19th century
Officers full dress
sporran. £35

A bronze magicians
lamp 7½ins. tall.
£28

A rock crystal ball
mounted on a rock
crystal column,
11ins.high. £450

An ivory and Shaba-
yama elephant. £475

Victorian brass
letter scales. £11

19th century bronze
figure of a greyhound.
£135

A Victorian lace fan.
£6

A Scrimshaw whales
tooth.   £25

A Shang Dynasty
archaic bronze wine
vessel.   £1,100

A set of Victorian
brass bankers scales.
£35

A George 111 carved
walnut tobacconists
shop sign 17ins. tall.
£115

A Victorian flat iron.
£2

Large iron Tsuba
3.25ins. diameter.
£30

A Ch'ien Lung
green jade bowl.
£4,000

A sawn and polished
vug with blue and
white agate bands.
£45

A Victorian stone garden urn 2ft.6ins.high. £40

A small Georgian four octave spinet 3ft 7ins., wide by John Broadwood, London. 1799. £275

A small Regency period terrestrial globe 14ins., diameter. £140

A Victorian glass ship under a glass dome. 9ins., high. £50

Large 18th century marble fountain in the form of a swan and four cherubs. £850

Late Victorian chair steps in oak. £18

A Victorian Zoetrope. £30

A Victorian Brougham coach. £500

A mid Victorian baby carriage. £45

A 16th century Italian full suit of armour made of bright steel. £1,250

A Victorian stuffed bird in a glass case. £14

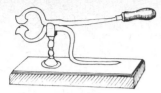

Pair of 19th century brass sugar cutters. £12

A Victorian bamboo hall stand. £18

A Georgian mahogany Butlers tray and stand. £80

A Victorian cutlery cleaner. £20

19th century ironwork plant stand. £15

A Flemish two manual harpsichord by Hans the Younger, circa 1690 £9,000

A late Victorian pottery elephant oil lamp 24ins., high. £85

Pair of late Georgian library steps. £100

Large Scottish spinning wheel in oak and pine. £35

Fine quality Gypsy Queen caravan. £600

A mahogany hoddmeter by Dolland of London. £65

Chippendale mahogany
kneehole desk on
bracket feet.   £510

Victorian mahogany
pedestal desk with a
cylinder top.   £125

Victorian mahogany
pedestal desk.   £120

Late Georgian satinwood
kneehole desk.   £625

Georgian mahogany
pedestal desk with pigeon
holes and drawers enc-
losed by a tambour
shutter.   £450

Chippendale mahogany
kneehole desk on ogee
feet, with writing slide
                £750

Sheraton mahogany
kneehole desk.   £550

William and Mary wal-
nut kneehole desk with
ebony arabesque mar-
quetry inlay.   £1,300

George I walnut knee-
hole desk with recessed
cupboard 2ft9ins.,
wide.   £1,100

Regency period padouk wood pedestal desk with brass edging to the top.
£220

Victorian oak pedestal desk. £70

19th century mahogany pedestal desk. £130

Victorian mahogany pedestal desk with brass drop handles. £135

Chippendale period mahogany serpentine front kneehole desk. £1,300

Military style camphor wood pedestal desk with brass handles and fitted top drawer. £340

Sheraton inlaid satinwood kneehole desk. £925

Queen Anne kneehole desk in walnut with a frieze drawer in the top moulding. £2,000

Late Georgian inlaid mahogany kneehole desk. £360

Georgian mahogany serpentine front chest. £750

Chippendale figured mahogany secretaire. £225

Hepplewhite secretaire chest in mahogany on splay feet. £225

19th century mahogany secretaire bookcase of inlaid satinwood with boxwood stringing. £360

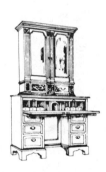

Georgian mahogany chest with secretaire drawer and cupboard top. £310

18th century serpentine front walnut writing cabinet. £1,300

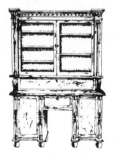

William IV mahogany secretaire bookcase. £230

Hepplewhite style secretaire bookcase in mahogany with glazed doors. £410

Sheraton style secretaire bookcase in mahogany with astragal glazed doors. £425

19th century brass banded
mahogany secretaire. £185

Georgian mahogany serp-
entine front secretaire
chest, 40ins. wide. £390

Late Victorian mahogany
secretaire chest on bun
feet, 3ft. 6ins. wide. £85

Georgian mahogany sec-
retaire bookcase 4ft.
wide. £460

Regency mahogany sec-
retaire bookcase veneered
in zebra wood. £1,100

Georgian tallboy in mah-
ogany with secretaire
drawer having canted
corners and ogee feet.
£385

Hepplewhite mahogany
secretaire bookcase with
cupboards below. £560

Fine secretaire bookcase
in satinwood inlaid with
urns and flowers. £2,600

Chippendale mahogany
secretaire bookcase with
shaped pediment and
ogee feet. £825

Edwardian inlaid mahogany suite on square tapering legs with spade feet.   £95

Edwardian ebonised suite with carved backs and tapered legs.   £80

Victorian button back suite with carved rosewood frames on cabriole leg supports.   £250

Louis XV style giltwood drawing room suite.   £375

Victorian mahogany rev-
olving piano stool on
platform base.   £20

Victorian revolving
piano stool in rose-
wood on paw feet.
£25

Victorian revolving piano
stool in papier mache.
£40

Regency period revol-
ving piano stool.   £45

Victorian footstool with
a beadwork cover.   £10

Victorian walnut
footstool on bun
feet.   £8

Regency period foot-
stool in rosewood. £20

Victorian mahogany
footstool.   £6

Georgian stool with
cluster column legs.
£100

Regency period carved
giltwood footstool. £100

Tudor period oak joined
stool.   £150

Hepplewhite mahogany
stool on reeded legs. £85

Hepplewhite mahogany
window seat.   £140

William and Mary foot-
stool in walnut.   £220

Silver coffee pot, London 1771. £1,000

George I plain cylindrical pot by Simon Pantin 1723, 28 oz. £2,250

George III silver coffee pot by George Smith and Thomas Hayter, London 1795. £475

Chocolate pot by Isaac Cooksen, Newcastle 1732. £1,000

George II Channel Islands hot milk jug by Guillaume Hardy Guernsey 1740. 9 oz. £1,500

George I plain bullet shaped teapot by Isaac Liger 1724, 13 oz. £750

Victorian plated teapot. £8

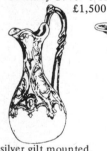

A silver gilt mounted, frosted glass wine jug by Charles and George Fox 1856. £130

A helmet shaped ewer with the full Royal armorials of Queen Anne by Thomas Boulton Dublin 1702, 47oz. £6,000

A Victorian plated cream jug. £10

George II plain pear shaped jug by David Willaume Jnr. 1730, 35 oz. £6,000

A George II flagon by Richard Bayley, 1737 £800

Beaker by Wakelin and Garrard London 1802, 3 oz. £100

Christening mug, London 1846. £30

Charles II beaker, London 1676. £1,000

George II coffee pot by John Chapman of London 1735, 27½oz. £500

George III silver coffee jug by Burwash and Sibley, London 1805, 25oz. £160

Swedish coffee pot by Anders Castem of Eksjo 1775. £3,500

Victorian coffee pot, 1845. £500

Victorian silver teapot, 18 oz. £45

George II bullet shaped teapot by Lewis Pantin, 1783 £1,750

George III silver teapot, 1818. £100

Cream jug by William King, London, 1768, 2½ oz. £75

George II silver jug by Charles Kandler, 1730, 52 oz. £3,000

Silver milk jug by Hester Bateman, 1786. £165

A William and Mary silver ewer, 1690. £750

Queen Anne mug, London 1702. £375

Christening mug, Birmingham 1861. £30

An Irish tankard, 1690. £500

A German silver tankard by Ulrich Schonmacher, 1580. £1,750

George III sauceboat by John Harris. £145

A reproduction George III sauceboat. £75

George II sauceboat. £200

Silver sifter spoon. London 1838. £10

Victorian grape scissors. £17

Georgian sugar tongs. £10

Georgian sugar nips. £17

Silver cruet with cut glass bottles. 1828. £95

Victorian egg cruet by George Fox 1865. £500

A Victorian silver egg cruet. 24oz. £75

George III Irish sweet-meat basket, 1794. 8½oz. £135

Pierced sweet basket with a blue glass liner, 1844. £80

Victorian silver cake basket, 16 oz. £40

Victorian silver sweet bowl, 6oz. £27

Silver punch bowl Guernsey 1700. £3,000

Hexagonal silver gilt sweet bowl, 1933. £55

SILVER

George III chamber-
stick, 1818, 9 oz. £100

George III chamber-
stick, 1801, 8 oz. £110

George IV chamber-
stick Sheffield 1828,
10 oz. £85

Heart shaped caddy
spoon 1825. £30

George III caddy spoon,
1802. £22

Bright cut caddy
spoon, Birmingham
1822. £25

Victorian leaf shaped
caddy spoon. £27

Late Georgian plated
tea caddy. £15

Set of three silver
tea caddies by John
Chivers of Birmingham.
£1,000

Victorian silver tea
caddy 1890, 11 oz. £35

Victorian plated
inkwell. £15

Victorian plated
inkstand. £22

George III silver ink-
stand by Samual Hennell
London 1813, 67 oz. £1,350

A Russian soup tureen
cover and stand. £850

An Italo-French soup
tureen and cover by J.
Beya, 1762. £4,250

Soup tureen and cover by Digby
Scott and Benjamin Smith, 1804,
324oz. £1,200

91

George III silver salt £25

Victorian silver mustard pot with a blue glass liner. £30

Silver mustard pot by John Emes 1803. £50

A Victorian silver vase, 6 oz. £14

A stirrup cup in the form of a hares mask by Emes and Barnard 1809, 11oz £1,000

Silver cup 1917 11 oz. £35

Two handled silver cup and cover by Paul de Lamerie 1737, 56 oz. £3,000

George II spirit kettle by Thomas Wright, 1754, 64 oz. £375

Sheffield plate spirit kettle and stand, 1860. £50

Kettle and stand by Ayme Videau, London 1735. £400

Victorian silver brandy warmer. £75

Victorian plated brandy warmer. £18

Silver brandy warmer 1937. £65

Small Victorian vinaigrette. £40

Victorian snuff box 1844. £75

Victorian silver match case. £5

Victorian plated syphon holder.   £6

George III silver gilt wine cooler by Paul Storr 1813.   £1,350

Sheffield plated wine cooler.   £90

Silver pepper caster, 1911.   £32

Victorian silver sugar caster, 4oz.   £22

Sugar caster by Simon Pantin, 1716.   £750

Silver caster by P. and W. Bateman, London, 1807. 3oz.   £100

George II silver salver London. 1759. 12½oz. £275

George III silver snuffer tray. London 1775.   £85

George III coaster by Peter and Anne Bateman, London 1798.   £60

Victorian silver smokers companion.   £35

Victorian silver frame.   £18

An Italian casket shaped foot warmer, 1730.   £2,500

George III silver bell.   £200

Victorian silver nurses buckle.   £8

George III wine label, 1790.   £14

Silver napkin ring. 1910.   £5

93

Victorian walnut chess table on a platform base. £35

Victorian black lacquered table inlaid with ivory. £30

19th century Japanese lacquer table with mother of pearl inlay. £45

Victorian bamboo pot stand. £5

Chinese Chippendale mahogany serving table. £115

Victorian mahogany cutlery stand. £12

Small Sheraton mahogany drum table on tapered legs with cross stretchers. £175

Small early 19th century mahogany drum table. £115

Victorian mahogany adjustable music stand. £25

Edwardian dark mahogany occasional table. £30

Victorian occasional table in rosewood. £25

18th century elm cricket table with shelf. £40

Adam style satinwood tricoteuse inlaid with garlands of flowers. £225

Louis XV ormolu mounted consol table with a marble top. £2,500

Georgian mahogany tea table on a tripod base. £105

Victorian walnut Gypsy table. £10

Early 19th century gilded tripod table with brass gallery. £55

Louis Philippe etagere in kingwood with Sevres plaques. £300

Victorian games table in walnut on a stretcher base. £45

Victorian mahogany bedside table. £15

Late Georgian mahogany architects table. £235

Syrian hardwood folding table inlaid with brass. £8

George III table with a painted porcelain top and ormolu mounts. £300

Victorian inlaid burr walnut tripod table 20ins., diameter. £45

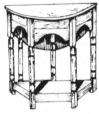

Charles II folding table in oak with plain turned legs. £200

Victorian papier mache tip top table. £60

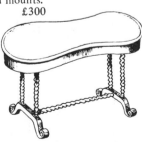

Victorian walnut stretcher table. £45

Regency period mahogany table with a parquetry top. £185

Regency rosewood card
table crossbanded in
satinwood.   £120

Edwardian inlaid mah-
ogany envelope card
table.   £85

Early Victorian rose-
wood card table with
a beaded frieze. £70

Hepplewhite mahogany
card table on tapered
legs.   £175

Regency rosewood card
table with brass inlaid
decoration.   £235

Victorian inlaid burr
walnut card table. £125

Regency mahogany card
table on fluted legs,
inlaid with satinwood.
          £95

Georgian concertina
action tea table in mah-
ogany on carved cab-
riole legs.   £320

Chippendale mahogany
card table with gadrooned
frieze on square legs
chamfered on the inside
edge.   £170

Queen Anne folding top
walnut card table. £450

19th century boulle flap
top card table with orm-
olu decoration.   £285

Queen Anne folding table
inlaid with flowers, on
carved cabriole legs. £475

Regency supper table in rosewood with a cross-banded top.   £160

Sheraton Pembroke table in satinwood, crossbanded in rosewood.   £400

William and Mary oak gateleg table.   £225

Victorian stripped pine Pembroke table.   £15

George III red walnut drop leaf dining table with club legs and pad feet.   £200

Victorian mahogany supper table.   £70

Late Georgian mahogany Pembroke table with boxwood stringing, on tapered legs.   £90

Late 18th century mahogany club foot envelope table.   £170

Georgian oak drop leaf cottage dining table.   £40

Small Edwardian inlaid mahogany Sutherland table.   £30

Regency mahogany dining table with concertina action, on turned and reeded legs.   £185

Victorian burr walnut Sutherland table with oval leaves.   £80

Regency sofa table with a crossbanded top, on lyre shaped supports. £650

18th century mahogany sofa table with D shaped leaves and crossbanded top. £775

Regency brass inlaid pedestal sofa table in rosewood. £475

Regency mahogany sofa table with a tooled leather top and flaps. £375

Regency rosewood sofa table crossbanded in satinwood with inlaid brass stringing. £400

Small mahogany sofa table on umbrella leg supports. £425

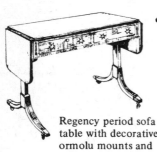

Regency period sofa table with decorative ormolu mounts and reeded legs. £325

Brass inlaid Regency sofa table in rosewood. £550

Regency ebonised sofa table with brass inlay. £300

Regency pedestal sofa table in mahogany, the edges and legs inlaid with coromandel wood. £300

Regency rosewood sofa table with crossbanded top on a stretcher base. £360

Regency rosewood sofa table with turned supports and splay feet. £400

Robert Adam giltwood side table.   £400

Italian carved walnut side table with pink marble top.   £275

Late 17th century Dutch table in laburnam wood.   £700

Regency pier table on tapered legs extensively decorated with curled paperwork of flowers and leaf designs. £1,250

Early 18th century Italian walnut side table.   £210

William and Mary oak side table.   £135

Elizabethan serving table in oak.   £225

Small red boulle side table with ormolu mounts.   £175

Victorian mahogany stretcher table.   £45

Regency mahogany consol table with dolphin front supports and brass gallery.   £475

Cromwellian oak side table.   £200

Carved and gilded Louis XV consol table with a figured marble top.   £450

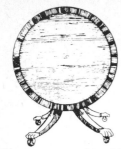

Regency centre table with a crossbanded rosewood top.   £350

Georgian mahogany supper table, the top carved with acanthus and shell ornament.   £200

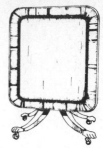

Regency rosewood, crossbanded breakfast table with brass claw feet.   £300

Late Victorian mahogany centre table on platform base.   £35

Regency mahogany drum table on tripod base with carved feet.   £475

Victorian burr walnut loo table on a centre column with cabriole shaped feet.   £150

Late Victorian inlaid walnut loo table.   £55

George II table and side table on carved cabriole legs with ball and claw feet.   £375

William IV mahogany table on a centre column with paw feet.   £70

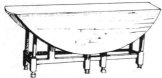

Irish wakes table in cherry wood.   £375

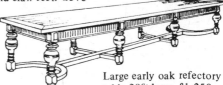

Large early oak refectory table 20ft.long.   £1,250

Georgian triple pillar mahogany dining table 12ft., long.   £950

19th century kingwood table with a tooled leather top.   £385

Regency brass inlaid centre table in rosewood. £750

Victorian mahogany centre table on a platform base with paw feet. £55

Victorian quarter veneered centre table in mahogany. £95

Victorian burr walnut marquetry loo table inlaid with birds and flowers. £500

18th century mahogany table on a carved tripod base. £120

Late Victorian walnut table inlaid with ebony. £80

Regency period rosewood drum top library table. 4ft diameter. £750

Large 17th century oak dining table. £375

18th century mahogany drum table. £750

Regency mahogany two pillar dining table. £325

Victorian mahogany telescope dining table. £35

Late 18th century sectional dining table in mahogany. £350

Early 17th century oak draw leaf table. £510

Edwardian red mahogany
sideboard.   £60

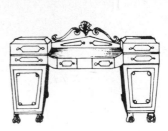

Early Victorian mahogany
pedestal sideboard inlaid
with ebony.   £85

Sheraton mahogany break-
front sideboard with satinwood inlay.   £400

Georgian mahogany bow
fronted sideboard 5ft.9ins.,
wide.   £340

Late Georgian mahogany
sideboard with a tambour
front cupboard. £450

Late Georgian concave
front mahogany sideboard.
          £300

Regency period maple
and satinwood sideboard
inlaid with ebony. £325

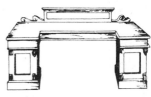

Adam period mahogany
sideboard on fine turned
legs.   £345

Early Victorian mahogany
pedestal sideboard.   £45

Late Victorian rosewood
sideboard inlaid with bone
and ivory.   £100

Hepplewhite mahogany
sideboard with a serp-
entine shaped front. £425

Georgian mahogany
sideboard 5ft6ins.wide.
                       £310

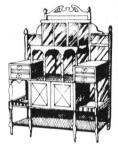

Edwardian mahogany
sideboard.   £50

Early 19th century small
inverted breakfront
sideboard in mahogany
5ft. wide.   £250

Regency period mahogany
sideboard on fine turned
legs.   £145

George III mahogany sideboard
inlaid and crossbanded in satinwood 5ft 3ins., wide.   £485

Sheraton period serpentine
fronted sideboard in finely
grained mahogany. £1,200

Regency period mahogany
sideboard on paw feet. £275

Victorian oak smokers companion.   £12

Georgian mahogany cutlery urn.   £90

Georgian mahogany apothecary box. £15

Regency period camphorwood writing slope. £50

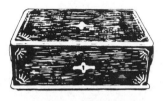

A brass bound Regency rosewood toilet box with fitted interior. £30

Victorian walnut writers companion.   £14

Small early 19th century inlaid mahogany tea caddy.   £25

George III mahogany table coaster.   £80

Victorian parquetry tea caddy with a glass liner.   £25

Regency mahogany specimen box. £90

A Victorian biscuit tin.   £5

Victorian walnut card box with brass fittings.   £12

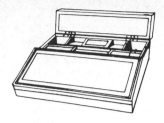

Regency rosewood
writing slope. £25

Late Georgian inlaid mah-
ogany knife box.   £50

Late Georgian apothecary
box complete with bottles.
£50

A Tunbridge ware writing
slope.   £45

A Victorian vanity case
in coromandel wood with
silver fittings.   £65

Victorian mahogany
cutlery box with a brass
carrying handle.   £8

A Tunbridge ware
jewellery box. £15

A Georgian mahogany
cheese coaster.   £50

A small 19th century
pony skin trunk. £25

Victorian games box
in walnut.   ·£75

Georgian mahogany
apothecary box. £60

Regency period brass
inlaid rosewood tea
caddy with glass liner.
£35

17th century oak mule chest. £135

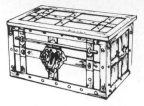

17th century steel banded treasure chest. £235

Georgian mahogany silver chest. £100

18th century Spanish carved walnut coffer. £275

17th century oak bible box. £65

Carolean oak dower chest with panelled front. £85

16th century oak hutch. £300

Elizabethan oak travelling desk. £60

17th century beechwood bread trough. £110

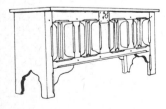

Tudor oak joined dower chest. £210

Victorian mahogany sarcophagus shaped cellarette. £70

Flemish Gothic buffet in elm. Circa 1500. £650

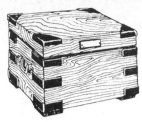

Brass bound camphor wood trunk with brass carrying handles. £60

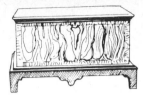

18th century walnut chest decorated with herringbone inlay. £155

19th century German ebonised cabinet of Baroque influence on carved scroll feet 7ft.5ins.wide. £1,400

16th century Italian cassone in carved walnut 4ft.10ins., wide. £350

18th century elm dough bin on square legs with stretchers. £65

17th century French cassette containing a multitude of secret drawers. £210

17th century iron treasure chest, the internal lock mechanism with eight moving catches. £285

17th century oak box on stand. £75

William and Mary period lacquered chest on stand. £485

Georgian country made oak bible box. £125

16th century oak bible box. £35

Late 17th century oak chest 4ft 2ins.,wide. £140

George III marquetry writing table. £375

19th century bureau plat in kingwood with ormolu mounts. £800

French walnut desk on cabriole legs with ormolu mounts and Sevres panels. £450

19th century inlaid satinwood bonheur de jour. £600

Regency rosewood library table with lyre end supports. £325

19th century boulle writing cabinet. £450

Louis XVI giltwood writing table with an adjustable centre flap. £750

Georgian walnut writing table. £475

Edwardian satinwood decorated writing table. £225

Georgian mahogany Carlton House writing table. £650

Victorian mahogany writing table with carved cabriole legs. £85

Louis XV style marquetry writing table with an adjustable writing slope to the centre. £500

Georgian Pembroke writing table with rise and fall secretaire. £300

18th century tambour desk with mock drawers in back and sides. 4ft.2ins., long. £375

Sheraton satinwood writing desk on tapered legs. £400

Edwardian mahogany table desk crossbanded in satinwood. £55

George III cylinder fronted mahogany secretaire. 3ft. 4ins. wide. £335

Victorian rosewood library table on a stretcher base. £80

Empire style mahogany bureau a cylindre with pierced brass gallery and marble top. 4ft6ins., wide. £365

Regency period rosewood writing table with drawers to the front, and pierced brass gallery. £170

Edwardian Hepplewhite style inlaid mahogany writing table. £85

Late Georgian satinwood and rosewood writing table. £525

19th century inlaid satinwood writing table. £310

Edwardian inlaid mahogany writing table. £45

Victorian burr walnut
octagonal work box on
carved cabriole legs. £50

Late Regency rosewood
teapoy inlaid with mother
of pearl.   £80

Tunbridge ware
workbox on splay
feet with brass
claw castors.
          £240

Regency work table
in yew wood on a
turned centre col-
umn and brass
paw feet.   £120

Victorian mahogany
folding top work table
on a shaped platform
with bun feet.   £80

Victorian burr walnut
sewing table on stretcher
base with carved
cabriole legs.   £95

Victorian walnut workbox
with a chess board top.   £60

Regency figured mahogany
work table supported on
carved splay feet.   £170

Victorian sewing table in
rosewood on a stretcher base.
          £80

Early Victorian burr walnut
work table with drop flaps.
          £115

Victorian work table in
mahogany on a centre col-
umn with platform base. £90

Victorian mahogany teapoy on a shaped platform base. £55

Victorian papier mache teapoy inlaid with mother of pearl. £85

Regency period brass inlaid rosewood teapoy. £235

Victorian teapoy in pollard oak on twist column supports and carved cabriole legs. £55

Victorian burr walnut work table with a chess board top. £125

Marquetry work table on turned legs with a single drawer and drop flaps. £125

Regency mahogany work table on turned column supports and stretcher base. £100

Victorian mahogany work table on turned legs. £50

Victorian mahogany work table on a centre column with shaped platform base. £55

Sheraton mahogany sewing table crossbanded in partridgewood. £230

Edwardian inlaid mahogany sewing table. £40

Sheraton cellarette of finely figured mahogany. £180

George III mahogany brass bound wine cooler. £275

George III mahogany cellarette on stand with brass carrying handles. £175

Georgian mahogany domed top wine cooler on square tapered legs. £160

18th century brass bound octagonal wine cooler in mahogany. £275

Chippendale mahogany cellarette with original decanters. £275

William IV wine cooler of figured mahogany on paw feet. £100

Hepplewhite oval cellarette in mahogany. £250

Sheraton mahogany wine cooler 22ins. wide. £230

Chippendale oval mahogany brass bound cellarette. £185

Sheraton mahogany cellarette on turned leg supports. £165

Sheraton period figured mahogany wine cooler inlaid with satinwood. £400

Victorian inlaid walnut three tier whatnot.   £50

William IV rosewood whatnot with twist supports.   £65

Victorian inlaid walnut corner whatnot.   £30

Late Georgian two tier whatnot in mahogany.   £95

Regency whatnot in rosewood.   £110

Regency four tier whatnot in mahogany.   £60

Early Victorian burr walnut whatnot.   £80

Sheraton mahogany whatnot with simulated bamboo supports.   £105

19th century red boulle etagere.   £120

19th century marquetry etagere.   £110

A Regency period rosewood whatnot.   £130

Hepplewhite mahogany whatnot.   £125

Early Victorian mahogany whatnot.   £90

Sheraton mahogany whatnot with two drawers.   £135

Georgian mahogany whatnot with cupboard base.   £90

Early 18th century oak clothes press. £175

Mid 17th century oak livery cupboard. £220

Georgian oak cupboard with four drawers to the lower section. £165

French provencal armoire in walnut. £285

17th century oak livery cupboard with panelled doors. £210

Victorian stripped pine wardrobe. £25

Early 17th century French cupboard in oak. £250

17th century oak cupboard. £425

17th century oak court cupboard. £320

French provencal armoire in walnut on carved cabriole legs. £200

Late Georgian finely grained mahogany breakfront wardrobe £160

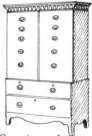

Late Georgian mahogany clothes press with mock drawers to the upper section. £85

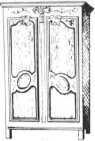

18th century French
provencal carved oak
armoire with steel
fittings.   £200

Late Georgian mahogany wardrobe with panelled doors and
two drawers to the base.   £75

Small William IV mah-
ogany cabinet with a
centre drawer.   £75

Georgian oak collectors
cabinet with key patt-
ern frieze.   £175

17th century oak
court cupboard.   £315

17th century oak clothes
press with two drawers.
                    £230

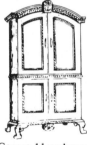

George 11 mahogany cupboard
on carved cabriole legs. £220

Elizabethan oak court
cupboard.   £450

Late Georgian mahogany
hanging wardrobe. £110

18th century Dutch
marquetry wardrobe.
          £1,000

Early 18th century oak
cupboard.   £285

Georgian mahogany linen
press on splayed feet. £75

CHAIR BACKS

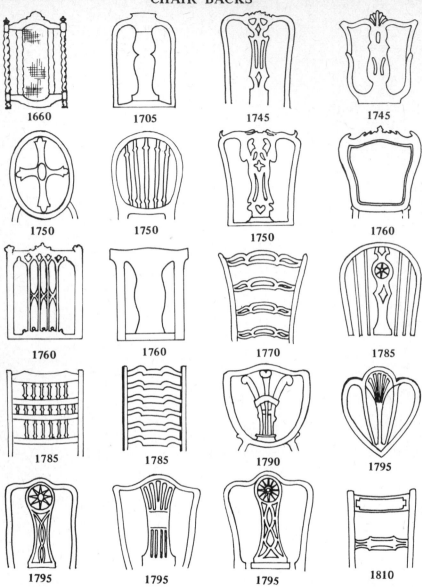

1660   1705   1745   1745

1750   1750   1750   1760

1760   1760   1770   1785

1785   1785   1790   1795

1795   1795   1795   1810

1660 Charles 11.	1770 Chippendale ladder back.
1705 Queen Anne.	1785 Windsor wheel back.
1745 Chippendale.	1785 Lancashire spindle back.
1745 Chippendale.	1785 Lancashire ladder back.
1750 Georgian.	1790 Shield and feathers.
1750 Hepplewhite.	1795 Shield back.
1750 Chippendale.	1795 Hepplewhite.
1760 French Rococo.	1795 Hepplewhite camel back.
1760 Gothic.	1795 Hepplewhite.
1760 Splat back.	1810 Late Georgian bar back.

CHAIR BACKS

1810   1810   1815   1815

1820   1820   1820   1825

1830   1830   1830   1830

1835   1840   1845   1845

1850   1860   1870   1875

1810 Thomas Hope 'X' frame.
1810 Regency rope back.
1815 Regency.
1815 Regency cane back.
1820 Regency
1820 Empire.
1820 Regency bar back.
1825 Regency bar back.
1830 Regency bar back.
1830 Bar back.

1830 William IV bar back,
1830 William IV.
1835 Lath back.
1840 Victorian balloon back.
1845 Victorian.
1845 Victorian bar back.
1850 Victorian
1860 Victorian
1870 Victorian.
1875 Cane back.

HANDLES

1550

1560

1570

1620

1660

1680

1690

1700

1700

1705

1710

1710

1720

1720

1730

1740

1550 Tudor drop handle.
1560 Early Stuart loop.
1570 Early Stuart loop.
1620 Early Stuart loop.
1660 Stuart drop.
1680 Stuart drop.
1690 William & Mary solid backplate.
1700 William & Mary split tail.

1700 Queen Anne solid backplate.
1705 Queen Anne ring.
1710 Acorn drop.
1710 Queen Anne loop.
1720 Early Georgian pierced.
1720 Early Georgian brass drop.
1730 Cut away backplate.
1740 Georgian plain brass loop.

HANDLES

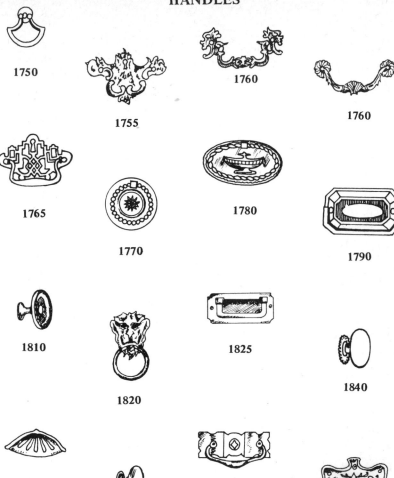

1750

1755

1760

1760

1765

1770

1780

1790

1810

1820

1825

1840

1850

1880

1890

1910

1750 Georgian shield drop.
1755 French style.
1760 French style.
1760 Rococo style.
1765 Chinese style.
1770 Georgian ring.
1780 Late Georgian stamped.
1790 Late Georgian stamped.

1810 Regency knob.
1820 Regency lions mask.
1825 Campaign.
1840 Early Victorian porcelain.
1850 Victorian reeded.
1880 Porcelain or wood knob
1890 Late Victorian loop.
1910 Art Nouveau.

LEGS

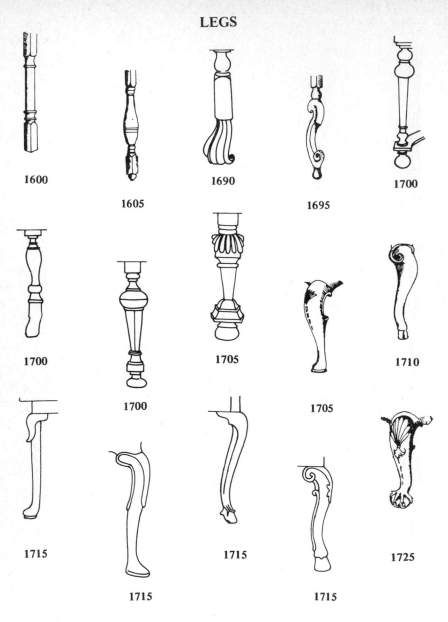

1600

1605

1690

1695

1700

1700

1700

1705

1705

1710

1715

1715

1715

1715

1725

1600 Elizabethan Turned.
1605 Stuart Baluster
1690 Spanish
1695 William and Mary 'S' Curve.
1700 Trumpet
1700 Portugese Bulb.
1700 Mushroom.
1705 Inverted Cup.

1705 Queen Anne Cabriole.
1710 Hoof Foot.
1715 Modified Cabriole.
1715 Pad Foot.
1715 Cabriole.
1715 Hoof.
1725 Ball and Claw.

LEGS

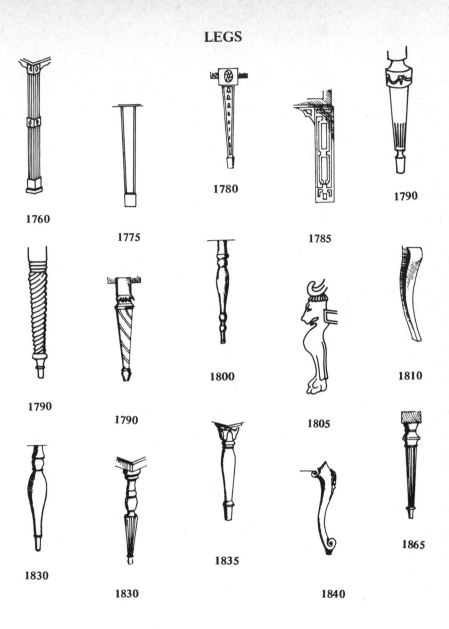

1760 Cluster Column.
1775 Square Tapering.
1780 Sheraton Tapered.
1785 Chinese Chippendale.
1790 Turned and Tapered.
1790 Tapered Scroll.
1790 Tapered Spiral.
1800 Windsor Turned.

1805 Lions Paw.
1810 Regency Sabre.
1830 Windsor Baluster.
1830 Turned and Fluted.
1835 Victorian Turned.
1840 Victorian Cabriole.
1865 Victorian Reeded.

PEDIMENTS

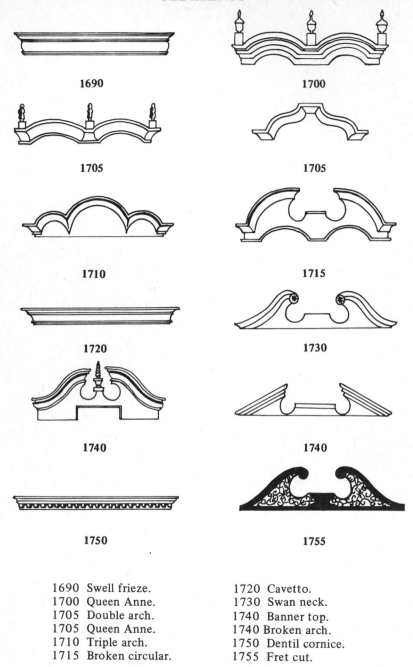

1690

1700

1705

1705

1710

1715

1720

1730

1740

1740

1750

1755

1690 Swell frieze.
1700 Queen Anne.
1705 Double arch.
1705 Queen Anne.
1710 Triple arch.
1715 Broken circular.

1720 Cavetto.
1730 Swan neck.
1740 Banner top.
1740 Broken arch.
1750 Dentil cornice.
1755 Fret cut.

INDEX

Apothecary box 104,105
Armchairs 32, 33
Armour 80
Armoires 114-115
Automaton Figures 74
Backs 116
Barometer 18
Beaker, silver 88,89
Beds, 29
Bedside table 95
Bell, silver 93
Bellows 78
Bible box 106,107
Bird cage 27
Blackamoor figure 19
Bookcases 22, 23
Bookshelves 22,23
Boats 75
Bonheur de jour 108
Bow 37
Bowl, glass 70,71
Bowl, silver 90
Boxes 104,105
Bracket clocks 50,51
Brandy warmer 92
Brass 24,25
Braugham coach 80
Bread trough 106
Breakfast table 100,101
Bronze 78,79
Bucket brass 25
Bureau 14, 15
Bureau a cylindre 109
Bureau bookcase 16, 17
Bureau plat 108
Butlers tray 81
Caddy spoons 91
Cake baskets 90
Cakestand brass 27
Candlesticks 26, 27
Canterburys 46
Capo di monte 36
Caravan 81
Card tables 96
Carlton House table 108
Carriage clocks 53
Cassette 107
Caster silver 93
Caughley 38
Cellarette 112
Centre tables 100
Chafing dish 27
Chairs 28,29,30,31
Chair backs 116, 117
Chaise longue 34,35
Chambersticks 91
Cheese coaster 104, 105
Chelsea 39
Chess table 94, 95
Chests 42, 43

Chiffoniers 58, 59
China 37, 41
China cabinets 57
Chinese porcelain 37-41
Chocolate pot 88
Claret jugs 69
Clocks 50-53
Clothes press 114-115
Coal skuttle 24, 25
Coaster silver 93
Copper 106
Coffee mill 24
Coffee pot, silver 88, 89
Commodes 47
Commode chests 44, 45
Console tables 94,99
Contents 78
Copeland and Garrett 39
Copper 24-27
Corner cabinets 54,55
Couches 34,35
Court cupboards 115
Cradles 21
Credenzas 58,59
Cribs 21
Cricket table 94
Cruet glass 68
Cruet, silver 90
Cupboards 114,115
Cups, silver 92
Cutlery cleaner 81

Cutlery urn 104,105
Davenports 62,63
Decanters 68, 69
Derby 38
Desk 108
Dining chairs 28,29
Dining tables 100, 101
Dolls 60, 61
Dough bin 107
Doulton 37-39
Dower chest 106
Dressers 64,65
Dressing tables 66,72
Drop leaf tables 97
Drum tables 94,100,101
Elbow chairs 30,31
Engines 75
Envelope table 97
Epergne 69,71
Escritoires 67
Etagere 95,113
Fire irons 26
Folding table 95
Fold over table 96
Footstool 87
Foot warmer 93
Fountain 80
Frame 93
Games box 105
Games table 95
Gateleg table 97
Globe 80
Gramaphone 74
Grandfather clocks 48,49
Grape hod 25
Grape scissors 90
Hall stand 81
Handles 118,119
Hans Sloane 39
Harpsichord 81
Hoddmeter 81
Howitzer 25
Imari 40
Inkstand ,brass 26
Inkwell, glass 71
Inkwell, silver 91
Inro 78
Introduction 9,10
Ivory 78
Jade 79
Jewellry box 105
Joined stool 87
Jugs, glass 68,69
Jugs, silver 88,89
Kettle, brass 24,25,27
Kettle, silver 92
Kinrande 39
Kneehole desk 82, 83
Knife box 104, 105
Lamp 26,27,81

Leeds 36
Legs 120, 121
Library table 101,108,109
Linen press 115
Livery cupboard 114
Longcase clocks 48,49
Loo tables 100,101
Lowboys 72
Lustre 68
Mantel clocks 52,53
Mennecy Magot 37
Metronome 78
Microscope 78
Milk pail 24
Military chest 73
Ming 39
Minton 39
Mirrors 76,77
Models 75
Monarchs 11
Mule chest 106
Musical box 74
Mustard pot 92
Napkin ring 93
Newhall 41
Nurses buckle 93
Paperweight 70,71
Pediments 122
Pedestal desk 82,83
Pembroke table 97
Periods 12
Phonograph 74
Piano stool 87
Pier table 99
Plant stand 81
Folyphone 74
Pot stand 94
Pram 80
Prattware 38
Preserving pan 24
Refectory table 100,101

Registry of Design 13
Rocking horse 60,61
Royal dux   36
Salver 93
Sauceboat 90
Saucepan 24,25
Scales 79
Scent bottle 70,71
Secretaire 84,85
Secretaire bookcase 84,85
Sevres 38
Serving table 94,99
Sewing table 111
Shells 78
Sideboard 102
Side table 99
Skillet 24
Small tables 94,95
Smokers companion 93
Snuff box 92
Snuff bottle 70,71
Snuffer tray 93
Sofa table 98
Specimen box 104
Specimen cabinet 56, 57
Spinnet 80
Spinning wheel 81
Sporran 79
Staffordshire 36-39
Steps 81
Stereoscope 79
Stools 87
Sugar cutter 81
Suites 86
Supper table 97
Sutherland table 97
Sweetmeat basket 90
Syphon holder 93
Tallboys 42,43
Tankard, silver 88,89
Tantalus 69

Tea caddies 104,105
Tea caddies, silver 91
Tea pots, silver 88,89
Teapoy 110,111
Tea tables 96
Toilet cabinet 66
Tongs, silver 90
Torcheres 19
Toys 60,61
Trains 75
Travelling desk 106
Treasure chest 106,107
Trivot 25, 26
Tricoteuse 94
Trunk 106,107
Tureen silver 91
Urn 80
Vanity case 105
Vinaigrette 92
Vitrine 57
Wakes table 100
Wall clock 53
Wardrobe 114,115
Warming pan 26,27
Washstand 66
Wedgwood 39,41
Whatnot 113
Whieldon 40
Wine cooler 112
Wine cooler, silver 93
Wine glass 70,71
Wine label 93
Window seat 87
Wood Ralph 37
Worcester 38,39
Workbox 110,111
Work table 110,111
Writing desk 109
Writing slope 104,105
Writing table 108,109
Zoetrope 80

THE END.

FINEM RESPICE.

Going for a Song.

Silver fiddle spoons - Gauge III - $35

Minton Parian figures, man, woman on couch. - £110.
Victorian   resemble marble